C000262567

Bluebells
and Gypsies

Bluebells
and Gypsies

Childhood memories of rural life in wartime Britain

Mary Daniels

HISTORY INTO PRINT

First published by
History Into Print, 56 Alcester Road,
Studley, Warwickshire B80 7LG in 2012
www.history-into-print.com

© Mary Daniels 2012

All rights reserved.

ISBN: 978-1-85858-342-6

The moral right of the author has been asserted.

A Cataloguing in Publication Record
for this title is available from the British Library.

Typeset in New Baskerville
Printed in Great Britain by
TJ International Ltd.

TABLE OF CONTENTS

Chapter 1

ESCAPE TO THE COUNTRY

*"There's a long, long trail a-winding
Into the land of my dreams."*
From *the World War I song* **by** *Stoddard King*

Fordrough was a long, new magical word. To me, as a diminutive young child, it was a memorable long word – and also a twisting, gritty, winding path to a blissful few years of my life.

The fordrough, 100 yards long, led to a massive, red brick farmhouse called Priest Park Farm where my family went to live in the early days of World War II when attacks drew dangerously close to the city of Birmingham.

We had been living in the Royal Town of Sutton Coldfield as it was known then, a gentle place in Warwickshire, and my father, as a journalist on *The Birmingham Mail*, travelled every day into the city on a Midland Red bus.

At five, I was too young to know what war meant but in a young child's sensory awareness of atmosphere I can still feel the sensation of doom that had swept through our home on that fateful day. At 11.15am on September 3rd 1939, we

Me aged five.

were all standing in the red-tiled hall of our Sutton Coldfield house, my father puffing solemnly at his pipe, when Prime Minister Neville Chamberlain's voice, emerging from the old wireless, chilled the air and announced – **"This country is now at war with Germany."**

As war and conflict loomed, the family decided to move away from danger into rural life until it was safe to return home.

Without that terrible day I would never have discovered the delights of country and small village life. We packed up and moved, my father, mother, brother Gerard, grandmother and myself to start with, later to be joined by another grandmother and various uncles, aunts and cousins, to the village of Chadwick End in Warwickshire.

At the end of the mysterious fordrough, as we arrived at the farmhouse with piles of luggage, large mushrooms greeted us in the front garden. They were taller than I was and I half expected a giant caterpillar to lean from one, smoking a pipe, just like the one I had heard about in bedtime reading from the book *Alice in Wonderland*. This really was wonderland.

The mushrooms were made of stone though and I later learned that they had been used at one time to prop up hayricks to keep them from the wet earth. Now they graced the centre of a lawn in the front garden of the farmhouse.

Oh! The smell of that earth in this strange place. Round the huge house was an old-fashioned garden full of lavender, hollyhocks, honesty, Canterbury Bells, numerous herbs, fruit and vegetables and huge, sweet-smelling old fashioned roses that almost pumped their intoxicating scent at us. The lavender was under each window so the scent wafted into the rooms when the windows were open in summer.

The porch of the farmhouse was surrounded by a clipped, privet hedge that made a complete archway over the door and there were even wooden seats provided on either side of the entrance by the huge front door in case callers got too tired waiting for the bell to be answered.

When we arrived, tired and anxious and loaded with a pile of cases and boxes, we were greeted by a large, warm and friendly lady who we learned was the farmer's wife. Her comforting presence immediately put us at our ease as we were invited through the giant oak front door that gave a friendly creak on its two enormous iron hinges.

The house was split into two halves. Half was for us and the other half was for the farmer and his family. Straight up the middle, dividing the two living areas and opposite the front door, was a grey stone staircase – with no carpet – the cause of many future painful knees in the next few years.

Upstairs, our allotted side had a long landing and just three very large bedrooms that were to provide shelter for my parents, my brother and myself and our maternal grandmother to begin with but for many more relatives and our paternal grandmother during the war years to come.

Our parents had a four-poster bed with curtains round and the other beds were all iron-framed, with highly polished bed-knobs screwed onto the four corners. Gerard and I used to unscrew the knobs on our beds, attach blankets across and screw them back in place to create our own four-poster beds or dens to play in.

Mother.

Chapter 2

EVERYDAY LIFE

"Water, water everywhere, nor any drop to drink."
From *The Ancient Mariner* **by** *Samuel Taylor Coleridge*

Exploring our new environment was like being in a foreign land. Firstly, there were no taps and no bathroom. Water came from a manual iron pump in the back yard and had to be drawn up from a well by working a long handle up and down until water flowed into metal buckets placed under the spout. Then it was carried to the kitchen for cooking and washing up.

In winter the whole pump was swathed in sacking to try and stop it freezing up but it was not always successful and we had to have a permanent supply of buckets of water in the house for emergencies.

In the corner of our little kitchen was a stove fuelled by coal or coke, with added wood from the farm. A giant metal kettle was kept on top constantly to provide hot water.

In the combined living room and dining room there was a large open log and coal fire. It was comforting to sit on the rug, making toast in the flames with home-made bread stuck on the end of a long metal toasting fork. When it was golden brown it was spread with farm-made butter and jam concocted from fruit gathered in the woods, fields and farmhouse garden. Toast has never tasted quite as good since those days.

In front of the fire was a thick rag rug that my grandmother had made. She took sacking, cut up old skirts, rags, left-overs from dress making and any spare material. It was cut into strips and pushed through the holes of the sacking with a metal bodkin, tying each piece into a knot. She also made them for the side of each bed to protect our feet from the shock of climbing out onto the cold linoleum on bitter winter mornings. Sometimes the rugs were just a jumble of colours. Others had scenes or animals in them, inspired by the colours of the materials.

The living room fireplace included an oven, heated by the flames, in which casseroles, bread and rice puddings could cook slowly throughout the day.

Butter was rationed for most people. Gerard (pictured below) and I used to make butter for our grandmother by putting rich farm milk into a jam jar with a tight fitting lid and then dancing round the room, singing and shaking the jars vigorously until the cream turned to butter for her morning toast.

Our three bedrooms also had fireplaces but these were never used unless we were ill. I remember having measles and the luxury of a real fire in the bedroom. Water in the bedroom was from flower decorated giant china jugs and basins on what were called washstands – wooden dressers with marble tops and a towel rail at each side. Washing in the morning was with cold water poured into the basin, unless it was really cold. Then a kettle was carried upstairs to top up the chilly wash.

Our maternal grandmother had an interesting variety of hot water bottles. There was a long, stone one, a round copper one a bit like a flying saucer and an ancient rubber one that gradually got longer and thinner until one night it burst and soaked the feather mattress. Born in the Victorian age, she never shortened her skirts and wore three – a long black one, under which she wore two underskirts, one red flannel and the other a shiny black taffeta. She had a tight bun at the back of hair fastened

Gerard.

with hair pins and always wore a black velvet choker round her neck and traditional gold-looped earrings in her pierced ears. Her long, black leather boots had little buttons all the way up the front and my job was to do up the buttons each morning using an ivory-handled button hook. Her serene face can be seen in the photograph on the right.

As I helped her to dress she used to sing the funniest songs. My favourite was one adapted from an old musical hall song of the early 1900's called *After the Ball was over, After the break of day*. Grandmother sang a comedian's parody of it:

Grandmother.

After the Ball was over
The lady took out her glass eye,
Put her false leg in the corner,
Locked up her packet of dye.
Put her false teeth in a saucer,
Hung up her wig on the wall,
And all that was left went to bye, byes,
After the Ball.

Bath time was a major event, hard work and usually about once a week. When the coast was clear, a metal bathtub was carried from the washhouse in the yard into the lounge and placed on the rug in front of the living room fire. Then buckets of water were laboriously carried in and poured into the bath. We all had separate bath days and the rest of the time we washed at the wash stands in the bedrooms. The washstand jugs and basins usually matched the chamber pot that lived under the bed – commonly called the "guzunder". There were no toilets in the house so we all had to use these at night and carry them to the outside compost heap in the morning.

The toilet itself was a walk round the house. We could go out of the front door and walk round two sides of the house through the flower and vegetable garden. Otherwise we went out of the back door, through the yard, past the pig sties and through a wicket gate into the garden.

There was the toilet. It was a shed with whitewashed walls and two holes side by side carved into a wooden board under which stood two buckets.

Spiders were a feature of the walls. They were not scary ones but had miniature bodies like full stops and long very thin legs that straddled the whitewashed bricks. I used to play games to see which spider could get into a brick without touching the lines.

There was no toilet paper in the country during the war. We had the luxury of numerous newspapers as my father was a journalist. My grandmother's job was to cut the previous day's Birmingham Mail and national morning papers into neat squares, puncture the corners and thread string through. It could be frustrating when an interesting story had been chopped in half leaving a tantalising snippet to read. Newsprint from the old hot metal presses had antiseptic qualities so they were quite hygienic. Buckets were emptied daily by the farmer onto a giant heap that also contained green garden waste, straw from the stables and sweepings from the cowshed. In time, when well rotted, it was spread on the fields to fertilise the crops.

The weekly clothes wash was done in the washhouse overlooking the back yard. A large wash tub was filled with hot water and the clothes were agitated with a washing dolly that was pumped up and down by hand. They were then fed through a mangle and pegged on lines in the garden to dry.

Although the village did not have the luxury of piped water, we did have electricity so a conventional electric iron could be used. The farmer's wife, however, still had heavy flat irons that were heated on the range and wiped clean of sooty smuts before pressing the clothes.

Chapter 3

THE VILLAGE SCHOOL

"When daisies pied and violets blue and cuckoo-buds of yellow hue
And lady-smocks all silver white do paint the meadows with delight..."
From *Love's Labour's Lost* by *William Shakespeare*

My brother Gerard and I were taken to the little village school. It stood in its own playground between a convent and a church about half a mile along the winding lane from the farm. There were three classrooms – infants, juniors and seniors.

I started in the infants' class. All the chairs and desks faced the front at which there was an open grate with a huge log fire. The teacher had the luxury of sitting by the fire to teach us. One of the teachers was a large nun from the convent next door. One day, as she sat on the chair reading to us, a chair leg broke in half and she went sprawling across the floor. That was when we had our first lesson in woodworm. The entire leg was riddled with small holes as the worms had eaten through the wood.

We were taught beautiful copperplate writing and every child could read by the time we moved to the next class. Writing was done with wooden pen holders with pen nibs slotted in. Each desk had a hole for the china inkwell and we took it in turns to be inkwell monitor. The wells had to be cleaned and filled with fresh ink every week and the monitor could always be recognised because of the week-long blue/black fingers.

We were also taught to read music using a giant Tonic Solfa chart pinned on the blackboard. Each day we sang a British song, many from the National Song Book which included folk songs from England, Scotland, Ireland and Wales. I have never forgotten those wonderful, traditional airs. They included *Annie Laurie, Early One Morning, Greensleeves, A Londonderry Air* and *Rule Britannia*. Many years later, BBC Radio 4 used to start its morning programme with the **UK theme**, a mixture of *Early One Morning* combined with several of those folk songs. It started my day, followed by the coastal weather forecast highlighting the places in the songs. The precious fifteen minutes ended with *Prayer for the Day*. That very special quarter of an hour was enjoyed by so many people before the powers

Our school.

that be decided to cancel its long run. It had played from November 23rd 1978 to April 23rd 2006. How sad that they ended it on Saint George's Day.

In the junior class there was a large wood-burning range. Pupils took it in turns to fill the enormous black kettle and make a cup of tea for the teacher. We all knew about using fresh water, warming the tea pot, adding fresh tea leaves (no tea bags then) and leaving the tea to brew before pouring. It was always served in a fine china cup and saucer with a silver spoon.

Sewing lessons used materials available during the war. Large racks of raffia hung at the front of the class and we would pull a long string of it out, thread it into a giant darning needle and then sew patterns and pictures into squares of sacking. It was amazing how inventive some of the children could be with such basic equipment and many Christmas presents for parents and relatives were made in those sewing sessions.

In the summer term, several children from farming families were allowed time off to help with the potato picking which was a vital crop during the war and entire families were employed in the backbreaking work.

My friend at the little school was a gypsy called Violet. Her eyes were violet and she was as wild and shy as her namesake that grew in profusion round her painted wooden caravan in the beech wood opposite the school.

Violet was a product of nature and came and went with the seasons as her family would move round to work as the different crops rotated. Her school life therefore was erratic. She learned little academically and came to us only in the spring term.

The highly painted, traditional caravan sat in the breathtakingly beautiful sea of bluebells that covered the wood in spring. I have never since seen such an incredible combination of colours as the carpet of bluebells beneath the new, pale green beech leaves interrupted occasionally by a milky way of delicate wood anemones. My love of small, wild flowers started here. I remember causing great mirth among the adults when I asked why those flowers were called wooden enemies when they were so delicate! Another one that puzzled me was the grape hyacinth in the farmhouse garden. I asked why they were called "grey pyacinths" when they were blue....

Violet's mother was probably quite young but to me she was older than the gnarled trees she lived under. Her long black hair, scraped back into a tight bun, and a deeply furrowed face were framed by the black clothes and black boots. She would sit by the door of the caravan on the step or on an old wooden chair outside. Both she and Violet smelled of kippers. I thought they must live on them. It was years later that I realised that the smell came from the smoky fire that was always burning by the door. Over this fire was a large black pot into which was popped anything that could provide a meal gathered from nature. The odd rabbit, birds, vegetables, nuts, fungi and wild herbs were popped in, with nettles from the ditches that they used as blood purifiers. Knowledge of plants was natural to them, and always, the mother said, for health's sake, she put a pinch of ginger in every meal.

I gave Violet the only book she had ever possessed. It was a small copy of Cicely Mary Barker's *Flower Fairies of the Trees*. She knew all about trees

and adored the book. I felt that she knew all those fairies personally. One of my favourites in that book was the fairy of the weeping willow tree, who swung from the branches overhanging the stream and "dipped her feet in the water cool".

Every weekend, the gypsies would leave the bluebell wood and go to market to sell the wares made by the mother during the week.

I would watch her as she sat on the wooden chair by the caravan door and transposed bits of hedge into sellable items. First were the clothes pegs made from two wooden legs, shaped at the base end and bound together with metal strips held together with a small nail.

The things I loved were the lilies. Small branches were cut from the hedge. Each piece of wood, stripped of its bark, was held tightly at one end. At the other, she pared gently down with a fine, sharp blade, almost like peeling a banana, so that each thin strip curled down as it was cut. Round and round she went until the end was covered with tightly curled petals. Then I was allowed to dip just the flower end into a metal bucket of bright orange dye that she had made from plants in the wood.

When the lilies were dry they were tied into bunches with fresh, pale beech leaf sprays and layed in a willow basket that she had also made from the willow trees that grew by the stream. Then, coloured scarf tied over her black hair, she and the family would go to the Bull Ring in Birmingham to sell the pegs and lilies at the Saturday market.

Sometimes Violet's father would come home with a small animal. One of the ways that they cooked rabbits or hedgehogs was to coat them with clay – fur or prickles covered – and pop them on the hot stones round the fire. The clay set in the heat, rather like the "chicken bricks" available now in expensive shops.

When the meat was cooked the clay case would be cracked open and with it came all the fur and skin, leaving succulent, tender meat with an incredible aroma.

Gypsies who come round to front doors now sell bought goods like elastic, plastic buttons and many things that are cheaper in the shops. Perhaps they cannot make those stiff, wooden flowers compete with the artificial silk and plastic ones now available. The Wildlife and Countryside Act has ruled out picking many of the flowers to sell. No wonder the gypsies have been tamed but I am sure that their wild spirits still linger among the few real bluebell woods that have survived the builder and planner.

Chapter 4

PIGS

"Odd things animals. All dogs look up to you. All cats look down to you.
Only a pig looks at you as an equal."
Sir Winston Churchill

Pig killing was as exciting a time to us children as bonfire night. The event was a ritual that I would abhor now but how we lapped it up then.

Pigs were our friends. We helped to feed them and scratch their wiry backs with a stick. When there was a litter we would watch entranced at the little pink line-up of snouts snuffling away as the sow, their mother, snorted with pride.

Gerard and I had our own pet pigs. They were called Oliver and Roland. Shakespeare perhaps would not have been amused at the allusion of his famous characters as swine. We loved them and could not and never did see their fate.

In the yard behind the farmhouse was an enormous metal barrel into which went everything, from peelings to scrapings from plates, all soaked with rain. This was used as food and liquid for the pigs and was poured daily into the giant trough in the sty. Sometimes there was even the odd match floating there but this brew, called swill, went down with them as if it was real ale.

When a pig was ready for the pot, the butcher from the village shop would come to shoot it humanely. The squeals were not from pain but from the indignity of being stretched on a slab. This for us started the ritual. A good fire would be lit in the farmyard and once the pig was dead it would be put on the fire to burn off all the bristles. It was as good as Guy Fawkes to us and we used to dance round the fire and sing, as the acrid smell pierced our nostrils.

Then the carving would begin.

At any pig killing in the village the first character to appear on the scene would be Old Liz with her metal bucket. To us she looked at least 100, with a face furrowed like a rocky mountain and her stockings in ridges to match round her ankles. Her aim was to get a bucket of blood. Her great age was probably attributed to the never ending supply of black pudding she brewed up, using blood, oatmeal, herbs and spices.

Every scrap of that pig would be used. The farmer's wife would turn the pig's head into a delicious savoury brawn, a spiced cold meat that we enjoyed with salads from the farmhouse garden and wonderful fresh bread baked in the farm kitchen by the farmer's wife or by my grandmother in our own little wood-fired stove.

Trotters were boiled in an onion and herb sauce to make a wonderful, savoury jelly. Joints were sold to the local butcher and the sides of bacon were salted and hung from the wooden beams, on huge hooks near the range in the farm kitchen, to catch the smoke from the wood fire. Slices of them crisped in an iron frying pan and served with freshly laid eggs from the chickens on the farm, were out of this world. The smell alone was something to remember. Vacuum packs of soggy, wet rashers from the supermarket and tasteless eggs bear no relation to the country bacon and eggs that we relished in those wonder days.

Potatoes were an important source of nourishment in the war. Anyone could grow them, and farms, town allotments and village gardens all invested in potato crops. Our farm had vast fields of them and when they were ready it was all hands on deck to dig up the crop, fill giant Hessian sacks and pile them onto the patiently waiting horse and cart to transfer them to the barns.

To encourage people to love them, the character Potato Pete was invented and he featured in cartoons, posters and numerous recipe books on how to make the old potato more interesting. We all drew our own cartoons of him at school and had competitions to see whose was the funniest.

Song of Potato Pete
Potatoes new, potatoes old
Potato (in a salad) cold
Potatoes baked or mashed or fried
Potatoes whole, potato pied.
Enjoy them all, including chips
Remembering spuds don't come in ships!

Chapter 5

THE POND

"Ducks are a dabbling, up tails all."
From *The Wind in the Willows* by *Kenneth Grahame*

At the end of the fordrough, near the brick barn, was a duck pond. In spring it was full of masses of frog spawn, strings of clear jelly filled with tiny black spots. These eventually became thousands of writhing tadpoles and our delight was to don wellingtons and wade into the murky water with jam jars fitted with a string handle. We would see who could catch the most tadpoles in one scoop of the jar. They were always put back to swim away and we followed their progress in the pond as they developed little legs before turning into frogs. Later in the year those frogs would be the natural predators of slugs in the farmhouse vegetable garden. The picture over the page shows a friend in the pool, preparing for the catch, with the enclosed cattle sheds in the background.

Major characters on the farm were Bill and Scandalous, two very large Shire horses that pulled the carts at haymaking and harvest. Scandalous was white and Bill was a deep, rich brown. One day, my brother climbed on the back of Bill for a ride. Bill had other ideas. He decided to take a drink in the pond and ambling across he bent his long, hairy-maned neck into the murky, duck-weed covered water. This created a slide down which Gerard shot into the pool. As he emerged, soaked to the skin and looking like a little green man he was the only person who could not see the funny side of it.

In winter, the pond froze over and provided us with a skating rink. We did not have the luxury of proper skates, just wellington boots or solid leather

shoes, but it was exhilarating fun and absolutely free. It was fascinating to hurl stones across the ice and hear the echo, almost like music, as it beat a rhythm across the frozen surface. The winters must have been colder because the pond was solidly safe to walk on and the ice must have been very thick. Many years later, my husband and I played the same ice music with our children hurling stones onto the lakes of our local park and listening for that echo of different notes.

Snow seemed so much deeper at the farm. Perhaps I was just so much shorter trying to wade through it. We would build a row of giant snowmen and then stand back and hurl snowballs at them to see who could knock off the hat, nose, twiggy arms or buttons, scoring a different mark for each one.

In summer, we learned the art of skimming stones on the water to see who could get the most bounces on the surface before the stone sank. That too had its own rhythm and music.

One of the farm labourers was always bent double, from continuous leaning over in the fields. When he brought Bill and Scandalous back to their stable for the night, he would stop first at the five bar gate in the field beyond the pond, bend even lower and start whistling. He had a particular tune that he directed at each horse. This had the effect of making them pass water before they went home, to keep the stable floor clean. We all knew the spot to avoid by the gate when we went into the fields!

The horses lived in a special stable attached to the end of the long barn where corn was kept through the winter. They were much larger than normal horses – to me they were giants – and their wonderful large heads would peer over the stable gate and stare at us with enormous, patient, brown eyes. In the day they worked hard, pulling wagons for the crops and also horse-drawn farming machines that ploughed and furrowed the soil ready for planting the cereals and root crops. As they went they naturally fertilised the soil.

Photograph shows me catching tadpoles while a friend looks on. She was Janet Whates, daughter of the Editor of The Birmingham Mail, who enjoyed coming to stay for a breath of country air. The five bar gate at the rear of the picture was where the horses were whistled to before going to bed.

Chapter 6

WILDFLOWERS

"To see a world in a grain of sand,
And a heaven in a wildflower."
From *Auguries of Innocence* **by** *William Blake*

My love of wildflowers, developed in those few years, has lasted all my life. At that time the fields, woods, hedges and ditches were strewn with different colours throughout the seasons and appeared each year like returning old friends, smiling in the sunshine and turning the fields into patchwork quilts and tapestries. They were even in the roadside verges and ditches on the way to school. The hedgerows in spring were brilliant with blossom and new

leaves. Tiny emerging green shoots of the hawthorn hedges were called bread and cheese and could be nibbled. There was no danger then of them being contaminated by fumes from passing traffic.

Part of my father's work was as a book reviewer. One day he came home with a bumper edition of the *Book of Flower Fairies* by Cicely Mary Barker. It contained the flower fairy books of all four seasons. Each watercolour illustration was accompanied by a poem. For me it was as if a magic door had opened. I learned all the poems, searched for the flowers and sometimes wrote my own poems too.

Christmas card.

A cat made from grasses, leaves and seed heads.

It is illegal now to pick many of the flowers, but in those days I was free to gather them and my grandmother taught me how to press them to make cards and bookmarks. Sometimes, the shape of the flower or leaves would suggest an animal or bird to create a picture. The Christmas card on the previous page is just one delphinium leaf, one young sycamore seed, a borage flower for the star and stamens for rays. The cat above is made from grasses, leaves and seed heads.

Our father's brother, Basil, and his family also lived in the country, far away in the south of England. Every year, my birthday present from them would be a shoe box, packed with wild primroses that they had gathered in the fields and woods near them. I filled every room in our half of the house with them, using tiny vases, egg cups, cups and saucers or jars. I also pressed some to return as cards. What a wonderful present.

One of the places we loved to walk or cycle to was the churchyard of the Church of England country church for the village, shown on page 20, that was built near the moated manor house, Baddesley Clinton Hall. It was filled every spring with a profusion of violets, cowslips and primroses. The farmer used to say that if you dug up a primrose, a cowslip would grow there and if you dug up a cowslip, a primrose would replace it. Sadly, those flowers are few and far between now in that little churchyard. Each spring though, even now, the wooded walk from the church to the Hall is a mass of bluebells and the ancient yew, seen on the left of the picture, is still there, guarding the secrets of the long history of the area.

The farmer taught us how to predict the weather with the scarlet pimpernel. These bright red splashes of colour grew along the edge of the cornfields. If the petals were open it would be fine. If they stayed closed during the day it was going to rain.

He also predicted the harshness of the coming winters by the amount of berries on the trees and bushes.

> Many haws, many sloes,
> Many cold toes.

Nowadays, that idea is dismissed but it always worked for him. Those farm-workers, who lived all their lives so close to nature, understood it far better than we can now with our fancy machinery, chemicals and distance from the soil.

He would also look up in the evening to examine the sky and know what conditions to expect the following day.

> Red sky at night, shepherd's delight.
> Red sky in the morning, shepherd's warning.

Seasons would be forecasted through the trees:

> If the oak is out before the ash
> We'll only have a splash.
> If the ash is out before the oak,
> We're sure to have a soak.

To the farm workers, even the way that both wild and farm animals and birds behaved, could be warnings of bad weather or storms.

Our farmer.

Chapter 7

BLITZ OVER COVENTRY

"We shall never surrender."
Sir Winston Churchill

The Warwickshire farm that our parents had chosen as a safe haven during the war turned out to be directly below a German bombing run for nearby Honiley aerodrome and Castle Bromwich. Gerard and I used to sit on the barn roof and wave enthusiastically to the pilots overhead, not realising that they were German bombers on their way to Birmingham.

On November 14th 1940, we heard a loud, very low sound of approaching aeroplanes. Excitedly, we watched as they swooped low over the farmyard.

That night the whole horizon turned a deep red. Gerard and I had gone to bed but were woken as the adults gathered to watch as the glow increased. We were too young to realise the real significance of what was happening, but once more, we sensed the anguish and desperation of those around us as we gazed at the increasingly reddened sky.

Everyone was talking about it next morning and it dominated the news on the wireless. This was the attack by German Luftwaffe over the city of Coventry nearby. We were to learn that the magnificent Cathedral Church of Saint Michael, the ancient tapestried hall of Saint Mary and the medieval Ford's Hospital had vanished overnight plus people's houses and shops and many hundreds of lives were lost.

Special services were held in the village Catholic and Church of England churches and all the churches of surrounding villages the following Sunday as many of the people killed had been relatives, friends and acquaintances of the local people.

Now, from the ashes of the historic ancient city, a new one has emerged. The modern cathedral of Saint Michael, designed by Basil Spence, stands next to the preserved ruins and tower of the old one, the outside wall dominated by Epstein's sculpture of Michael the Archangel. Next to it, in the roofless preserved ruins, stands a cross made from charred roof timbers from the bombed remains and placed on an altar made from the rubble. The words **Father Forgive** are carved on the sanctuary wall, a potent reminder of man's inhumanity to man. Another cross, made from three ancient medieval twisted nails taken from the wreckage, has become the symbol of the new City of Coventry's ministry of reconciliation.

Many years after that fateful bombing raid, when I was married and with children of my own, I went with my husband, John, to a performance in the new Cathedral of Saint Michael of Benjamin Britten's *War Requiem*. The work had first been commissioned and performed for the opening of the restored cathedral in May 1962, and has had many performances there since then. As we listened, spellbound, to the moving music of the Latin Mass combined with the war poems of Wilfred Owen, I was taken back to that fateful night when history was demolished and our peaceful rural retreat was overshadowed by that burning horizon of horror.

At the little village school, that up till then had seen nothing of the war, we all had to have a gasmask practice and march into the long corridors of the convent next door, which were to be used as an air raid shelter. Every day we had to take our gasmasks, in a box with a string shoulder strap, and keep them close by, each one labelled with our own name. They were never needed but we had regular practices to put them on in case the dreaded air raid siren sounded. That too was rehearsed with a terrifying wailing sound. Younger brothers and sisters of village children, who were too young to start school, also had gasmasks. They were in the shape of Mickey Mouse heads with separate eye pieces and a nose. To me they looked more frightening than the real ones we had. When we put the masks on we had to try breathing in them and they made a most extraordinary noise, like great

bellows, that reminded me of the calves breathing heavily in the misty fields or over the doors of the cow barns. I can remember wondering if they would provide special gas masks for the cows and horses too. The other things that we all had to wear were Identity Discs. These were aluminium bracelets engraved with our name and address. They shone like silver and I was very proud of mine. I think they cost a shilling each, the equivalent of 5p now.

One day a group of men arrived to work on the farm. They were Italian prisoners of war. Some of them could speak a little English, many could not, but we made friends with them. They were gentle people and skilled with their hands. I was given the most wonderful wooden birds and animals that they carved from fallen branches or bits of wood left over from the stack of firewood cut for our fires at the farmhouse. I wish I had kept those marvellous little souvenirs of my war days.

One day we were crossing the main road in the village on the way to school. Men were digging up the centre of the road and fitting what looked like giant eyes. I asked what they were doing and they said they were putting eyes in so that the Australians could keep an eye on us from the other side of the world! I almost believed them and I certainly avoided those eyes when I skipped to school. They must have been the first cats' eyes that were installed in every main road to guide cars after black out as they drove with dipped headlights to avoid being seen from overhead planes. They had been invented before the war, in 1934, by Percy Evans, and were first put in some roads in 1935, but came into their own in the 1940's in wartime and are now still part of our roadways.

The news on the wireless was not on every hour as it is now. It was a major feature at midday and once in the evening. When it started the rule in our house was that everyone fell silent. Even now I cannot speak during the news. My father, as a journalist, had to know what to write about in The Birmingham Mail's daily editorial comment on world and local affairs, known as the Leader. There was no television or other means of communication and the Home Service News on the wireless was vital to his work.

Next morning, he would cycle to the station a mile and a half away to catch a steam train to the city. By the time he had arrived he had written his leader in a notebook, ready to type it onto the old office typewriter. Then it was handed in to be set on the hot metal printing machines, proof read, corrected, reset and printed in the first edition of the day. Modern computer technology has abolished a swathe of skilled workers who were part of the old newspaper industry. Nowadays journalists can sit at home and send the copy via a computer directly to the printing machine. My father would have been amazed at the technology that has overtaken his skills since then.

One item that made the news on our farm was the crashing of a Messerschmitt, a German war plane, in the cows' field. No cows were hurt. No mention was made to my brother and me about the fate of the pilot but I presume he died. The field was put out of bounds to children for a long while. It was years later, after we had left the farm, that the engine of the plane was recovered from deep under the ground, disguised by natures' healing plants and flowers.

Chapter 8

THE PARISH

Baddesley Clinton Hall.

"Oh, you'll never get to Heaven in an old Ford car...."
Traditional camp fire song

Next to the convent and the little village
school was the Catholic Church of Saint
Francis of Assisi. It was an appropriate name
as it stood in a country lane surrounded by the
birds and wild animals that Francis loved so
much.

My brother and I walked along the country
lane to the church on Sunday with our parents,
grandmothers and aunts. The photograph on
the right shows our paternal grandmother in
the walled farmhouse garden.

It was a traditional little church with long
wooden pews. The sanctuary wall behind the
altar was painted with numerous saints. At first
they seemed different but on examination they
all had the same face. They all featured
Marmion Ferrers, a 19th century benefactor of

Grandmother.

the convent from the local mansion house, Baddesley Clinton Hall, who used to walk up the lane from the Hall to Saint Francis's Church to serve at the early morning Mass. Marmion's own wife, Rebecca, was a talented artist and she had painted the murals putting her husband's face onto each saint. She also painted the fourteen Stations of the Cross that are still round the walls of the church. Sadly, the murals of the saints have now been painted over but for us they were a fascination. An oil painting of Marmion Ferrers was kept on the wall of the convent parlour, showing him bearded and with a cloak, standing in front of his moated Hall.

Each Sunday, when we were at Mass, just as the priest reached the pulpit, the door used to swing open and in rushed a latecomer who puffed and panted up the aisle to the front bench. She was a local from the village whose dramatic entrance we anticipated with glee as every Sunday she was dressed in the colour of vestments of the day. On the feast of a martyr her hat and coat were a flaming red. In Lent she wore purple and on ordinary days everything was green. We always hoped that one day she would get it wrong, but she never did.

Nuns from the convent had a special room overlooking the sanctuary from which they attended services. The congregation could not see them but we heard their singing, which was always much better than the efforts from the church.

One Sunday evening Father Dale, the parish priest, was celebrating the church service of Benediction. Suddenly his prayers got faster and faster and the hymns increased in speed. The poor nuns were breathless trying to keep up with him and the congregation was bemused.

As the last verse of the final hymn was being sung, the priest leaped down the Altar steps and raced out of the church, arriving back shortly red-faced and panting.

"I'm so sorry," he announced to the congregation, "half way through Benediction I remembered that I had left the lights of my car on and black-out restrictions had started."

During the war it was illegal to show any light in the street. Car lights were dipped when driving and even the lenses of torches had to be half covered with black paper to prevent them from being seen from above by a passing enemy plane. As the priest apologetically explained his predicament it was the first time I had ever heard people actually laughing in church. His shiny black car was a feature of the village as very few people in those days had one of their own. Most people walked or used bicycles and even the cycle lamps had to be covered across the top half of the lens to obscure them from the sky.

My brother Gerard was being trained as an altar server. He was very thin and slight. In those days, the altar had an Epistle side and a Gospel side. The words of each were read from one very large book on the altar and it had to be carried, complete with stand, from one side of the altar to the other between readings. Gerard, wearing the altar boy's black cassock and white cotter, reached up on tip toe to get the book, his little face peering over the large leather cover. Suddenly he staggered and fell down the altar steps dropping his heavy burden, which bounced noisily down each step. My mother was horrified. After Mass, Father Dale said to my parents, "Gerard has now qualified. He has done the belly-flop and it will never happen again."

When I made my first Communion with several other children from my class at school, my grandmother made me a special white dress (shown in the photograph on the right). Round the collar she embroidered my favourite coloured flower, sky blue forget-me-nots. I shall never forget that dress, those flowers or the wonderful grandmother who made me so many things with her skilled fingers, especially as materials were so hard to find during the war. After the Mass the nuns gave us a special Communion breakfast in the convent. We sat round tables covered with beautiful, embroidered cloths that the nuns had made. We were amazed and impressed to find that the feast included a large fruit cake – cake at breakfast time was something we had never been given before and it made it very special.

Three years later the same children were Confirmed. Bishop Bernard Griffin of the Archdiocese of Birmingham, who later became Cardinal Griffin, performed the ceremony. Out of all the girls being confirmed I was the only one who did not take the Confirmation name of Therese. It was already my middle name so I chose the name Agnes and Bishop Griffin showed surprise and relief when he heard that someone had chosen a different name.

My first Communion.

There was no fruit cake that time but I can remember going out into the fields at the back of the farm after the ceremony and walking through the mass of wild flowers that were so prolific at that time in early summer. By then I knew all their names and colours and was in love with them for life. No amount of giant, exotic garden blooms can compete for me with the tiny, delicately coloured flowers of the fields and woods that appeared in their own special time throughout the year. Sadly, many fields of wild flowers have now disappeared with the progress of farm technology. We have to rely on what the poet William Wordsworth called, "the inward eye", to recall those vast tapestries of seasonal colour.

Every June, the church held a procession through the gardens of the presbytery. The priest would carry a host, housed in an ornate gold monstrance, along the paths as the congregation processed and sang. Four altar servers, one to each corner pole, held up an embroidered canopy to shelter the priest as he walked. It was the job of the girls to be strewers. We gathered petals from roses, peonies and other scented flowers from the gardens and piled them into willow baskets like the ones made by the gypsies in the wood. Then we had to walk backwards in front of the priest and strew the petals on the path for him to walk on. Being small, I was near the ground and could smell the heady scent of the petals as he crushed them under his feet. As everyone else prayed, I just hoped I would not fall over as I was trying to walk backwards along a curvy, stony path and throw the flower petals as I went. If it was a windy day it was harder both for the strewers to aim for the path and for the servers to steady the flapping canopy.

The graveyard round the church was also full of wild flowers and sometimes a little field-mouse with tiny, beady black eyes could be seen scurrying near the path. There was always the song of birds and the hum of bees in summer and many butterflies flitted through the grass and often landed on the stones as if to read the names of past parishioners who rested in that quiet and peaceful place.

Father Dale frequently visited the farm to see my grandmother and enjoy a chat and a meal with the family. On the mantelpiece he kept Mother Abbess. This was an enormous, curly, wooden pipe that rested on a tin of tobacco. He would arrive, relax in a chair by the fire and load the pipe, puffing loudly between each flash of the match as he lit it. In those days, most people who came to the house smoked. The dangers were not recognised and as conversation usually took place in a draughty room, round the fireplace and open fire, the smoke was drawn automatically up the chimney and did not pollute the air as it does in our modern, tightly sealed, centrally heated rooms without chimneys and with all the draught entrances sealed.

There was always a problem of flies in the summer due to the proximity of the farm buildings and my mother used to buy sticky fly papers from the village shop to hang from the light and catch the flies before they landed on the table. Father Dale one day decided he could make a fly paper himself. He arrived for tea complete with a roll of paper covered in golden syrup and a piece of string to hang onto the light fitting. It worked well and the flies devoured the syrup, getting their feet stuck in the process – that was until the room warmed up as we poured tea. Slowly, the golden syrup melted and landed, complete with flies, into the jug of milk on the table. The flies began to swim away in the milk and mayhem ensued as mother tried to rescue the food.

The priest's presbytery was next door to the convent and the school. My family were very close to the convent nuns because one was the youngest sister of my father and she was also my Godmother. Some years after we left the farm she became Mother Abbess and held the post for more than a quarter of a century. We were all fond of those wonderful nuns who were so much a part of the school, the village and the parish. When we were there they taught in the school, kept poultry, grew all their own vegetables and fruit in the convent grounds and also provided flowers for the church altar. Many of the nuns were artistic and throughout our lives we received hand-painted pictures and cards and embroidered cloths.

Over the years, with age and ill health, the number of nuns diminished. On January 8th 2011, the closure of the Convent of Poor Clares was recorded with a special Mass in the church celebrated by the Archbishop of Birmingham, Archbishop Bernard Longley, with a packed congregation and many diocesan priests who had known the nuns. After 160 years at Baddesley, the last few nuns of the convent were leaving this peaceful and tranquil place of prayer. Their final act for those present was to give everyone some of their delicious jams and jellies that they had produced for so long, marked with a special label saying FINAL BATCH.

My aunt and Godmother, Mother Paula, outside the convent door.

Chapter 9

HARVEST TIME

"Oats and wheat and barley grow."

Harvest time was a social event for the whole village.

Men would arrive with guns, ostensibly to help with gathering the corn but really in the hope of bagging some rabbits to eke out the wartime rations.

Cutting the corn would start from the outside, a tractor and cutter chopping the oats, wheat or barley and dropping it in bundles called sheaves. The job for everyone, including the children, was to gather the sheaves and arrange them into stooks. These were groups of sheaves standing up, three on each side and one at each end. They were then left to dry in what they hoped would be sunshine, before bringing them into the barns. They were bigger than I was but it was such fun struggling with giant bundles of corn and we were never stopped for health and safety reasons. It was all hands on deck however large, old, young or small we were.

Round and round the tractor went, getting further into the centre of the field. As they went, the rabbits hiding in the corn raced further and further into the centre until the very last of the corn fell. Then every man with a gun started to shoot the rabbits that fled in all directions. How nobody was killed I shall never know. Our modern Health and Safety Officers would have had a field day – literally.

Once the animals were disposed of and the clever ones had managed to escape, they were gathered up. Long poles were cut from the trees and the rabbits hind legs were tied together and strung from the pole. Men carried the poles, one each end, with their booty hanging head down, until they were counted, shared, put in bags and taken home for dinner.

We used to sing this song as they tried to shoot the rabbits. *Run Rabbit Run* was a popular song during World War II.

On the farm, every Friday
On the farm, it's rabbit pie day.
So, every Friday that ever comes along,
I get up early and sing this little song.

Run rabbit – run rabbit –
Run! Run! Run!
Run rabbit – run rabbit –
Run! Run! Run!
Bang! Bang! Bang! Bang!
Goes the farmer's gun.
Run, rabbit, run, rabbit, run.

Run rabbit – run rabbit –
Run! Run! Run!
Don't let the farmer have his fun!
Fun! Fun!
He'll get by without his rabbit pie
So run rabbit – run rabbit –
Run! Run! Run!

My grandmother's rabbit pie was memorable. Inside a raised pastry case she would put a mixture of rabbit meat, herbs, vegetables, seasoning and boiled eggs. When the pies were cooked and allowed to cool, slices would show a mixture of the eggs, meat and other ingredients all set in a natural jelly from the meat, and the smell and taste were amazing. Casseroled rabbit eaten hot was also delicious served with home grown vegetables from the farmhouse garden.

Haymaking was different. After the hay had been cut and left to dry in the fields it was collected on hay carts drawn by the Shire horses Bill and Scandalous. We were allowed to ride on top of the piled hay cart and have a ride back to the farmyard barns. One year Bill went too near the ditch and we were tipped off but it was all part of the fun.

The hay was stacked into Dutch barns, which were open buildings topped by curved, corrugated iron roofs. To Gerard and me they were special secret places. There was always a ladder against the hay and we could climb up, lie very quietly on the comfy hay, and watch the swallows zoom in to build mud nests, rear and feed their young and then see the young birds fledge and fly away.

One day we were up there making not a sound when the farmer decided he needed the ladder. We were stuck on the hayrick in forbidden ground. When the coast was clear Gerard threw down mountains of hay from the top until there was enough for us to jump down and have a soft landing. We were fine but the farmer must have wondered what damage he had done when he took away that ladder.

Foxes were the enemy of farmers and they multiplied in the surrounding woods and hedgerows. However appealing they looked in pictures and in children's story books, they wreaked havoc on the farm.

Adjoining farms to ours, that kept sheep, suffered from the loss of lambs in spring when foxes got into the fields. Our own farm had chickens and ducks and sometimes in the morning we would find a sad trail of feathers when a fox had visited the farm in the night.

To control them, there was a fox hunt on Boxing Day every year, to which everyone in the village went to wave off the huntsmen. It began very early in the morning and in my memory it was always misty.

One of the songs from The National Song Book that we used at the village school was *D'ye ken John Peel?* – a traditional fox-hunting song, and we all sang it loudly as we watched the gathering of the horses and dogs and the hunters wearing red coats. The breath of the dogs, horses and people formed clouds in the mist, adding an extra air of excitement to the occasion. Then, when the hunt was ready to go, one of the red-coated men on the leading horse would blow a large horn that echoed across the village. This occasion, that at one time was an essential part of country life in England, can no longer take place now with the banning of fox hunting by the government but art and literature abound with memories of the event.

John Peel, subject of the song, was an 18th century Cumbrian farmer and huntsman with his own pack of fox hounds and the original version was written by his friend John Woodcock Graves (1795-1886). "D'ye ken" is Northern English and Scottish dialect for "Do you know":

D'ye ken John Peel with his coat so gay?
D'ye ken John Peel at the break of day?
D'ye ken John Peel when he's far, far away
With his fox and his hounds in the morning?

For the sound his horn brought me from my bed
And the cry of the hounds which he oft times led
Peel's "View Halloo!" would awaken the dead
Or the fox from his lair in the morning.

Chapter 10

BIRD-WATCHING

"Among the dwelling framed by birds
In field or forest with nice care,
Is none that with the little wren's
In snugness may compare."
From *A Wren's Nest* by *William Wordsworth*

Just as I had a fascination for the wild flowers, Gerard's was for birds and his love of bird watching lasted him a lifetime. His birthday presents were bird books and he could recognise and name all the birds on our Warwickshire farm.

The farmer taught us a lot about them. I always remember him giving us a lesson on how to distinguish a crow from a rook.

"If you see a rook on its own, it's a crow.
If you see a lot of crows together, they're rooks."

Many of the tall groups of trees on the farm housed little villages of rooks. The rookeries were built high up in the top of the trees – many nests close to each other – that waved precariously in high winds but never fell. As they nest early, before the leaves cover the tree tops, their activities could be watched easily. The rooks love to socialise and make a tremendous noise, especially when they

perform communal flights which are such fun to watch. They do eat corn but they also eat the pests that invade the corn. In 1424 King James I of Scotland decreed that rooks should be exterminated from his kingdom to protect the corn. His scheme failed because the pests that would have been eaten by the rooks destroyed the corn crops. Interfering with the balance of nature is not always a good idea.

On a hot July day magic filled the air. We would lie on our backs on the grass and see the skylark as it tried to climb to heaven in the blue sky, letting down trails of silver notes that filled the air. Skylarks are becoming rarities these days but we took them for granted then. One of the songs we sang at the village school was a setting of the Shakespeare poem from his play *Cymbeline, Hark, hark the lark at Heaven's gate sings*. I understood that song perfectly because we knew the birds personally. At that time I had not heard Ralph Vaughan Williams' wonderful violin music for *The Lark Ascending* but it is now one of my favourite works. When I hear it the hypnotic melody takes me back to those days in the fields, just watching, listening and gazing into the sky as the bird climbed vertically higher and higher, then suddenly plummeted to earth, still singing, until it disappeared somewhere in the undergrowth. We were warned to be careful when walking because larks lay their eggs on the ground and we did not want to crush them.

Other birds that we loved were the green woodpecker, always busy in the trees round the farm, and the tiny little wren with a lot to say that nested in the ivy on the wall below my bedroom window. Many years later my love for the wren inspired me to compile an anthology about it, called *The Farthing Bird*. At that time it was the logo for a local hospice so the teeny bird of my childhood from the weeniest of coins raised a lot more than a farthing for a good cause.

When we were at the farm, the small farthing coin, which was a quarter of a penny, was still in circulation and featured a wren on the opposite side from the King's head. It did not go very far then but my grandmother once said that when she was young and had four children a farthing bun cost a whole penny. Four buns for a penny must have seemed a lot at that time. How times have changed.

In the roof of the enclosed red brick barn on the farm lived barn owls. Their strange, eerie cries in the night were somehow soothing and if I was lying awake, especially if I was ill, their wild cries were like a lullaby.

In those days the cuckoo was a frequent visitor in spring. We knew that it layed its eggs in other birds' nests, relying on other species to foster her young, but even so we loved to hear her call and knew that fine weather and summer would be on the way.

At the village school we used to sing a song about the cuckoo.

> In April, I open my bill.
> In May, I sing night and day.
> In June, I change my tune.
> In July away I fly.
> In August, away I must.

If we heard a cuckoo's call after August we knew it was a human mimic.

Down by the stream at the far end of the farm land, where we paddled and fished for sticklebacks, we were sometimes treated to a spectacular flash of the brilliant blue-green back and bright orange underside of a kingfisher. They would catch tiny fish, tadpoles or insects to feed their young that perched on a branch by the stream. We had to keep very still to see them as they are shy birds. The farmer told us that birds of prey did not touch them because even though they looked beautiful they tasted horrible.

Pied Wagtails were amusing to watch as their long tails bobbed up and down when they walked. We were taught John Clare's poem, *Little Trotty Wagtail* at the school and it was so descriptive of their funny little walk. John Clare has remained one of my favourite poets because he encapsulated, many years before, the heart of the countryside in which we were immersed and that later was to change for ever.

In the wood we would often see Jays. Their tiny wing feathers had blue and white stripes and I still have the little blue Jay's feather that our father wore tucked in the band of his trilby hat, even after the war when we returned home. As he travelled on the bus into the city in those post war days, always wearing his hat, he too had that little reminder of our magical country life.

The profusion of birds, moths, butterflies, wild creatures and flowers that made up the colourful tapestry of our leisure days is a memory that can never be forgotten. Fields and hedgerows were packed with seasonal colour. Even the corn and hay fields, before weed-killer sprays were brought in, had their own special tapestry of colour. Sky blue cornflowers, red wild poppies and brilliant white ox eye daisies were nature's own way of spreading its banner of the red, white and blue that spurred us all on to fight for freedom.

Flowers for me had personalities. There were the shy ones, pale and tiny, that hid in woods and undergrowth and peeped out. Then there were the brazen, highly coloured ones that flaunted in the sunshine as if to shout, "Look at me". Some were prim, staid and upright and others were just a total, abandoned mess but loveable with it.

Herbs were mysterious. Many years later, I studied the legends and history behind herbs and wild plants that have dominated our civilisation since man arrived.

The most popular bird in the war was one that we did not see on our farm. It was the blue bird, made famous by the singing of wartime Forces pin-up and singer Vera Lynn:

> There'll be blue birds over
> The white cliffs of Dover,
> Tomorrow, just you wait and see.
> There'll be joy and laughter
> And peace ever after,
> Tomorrow, just you wait and see.

Every adult and child in the 1940's knew the song and that little blue bird epitomised all the wild creatures that we fought to treasure and protect in our war-torn world.

Chapter 11

FRUIT AND NUTS

"Season of mists and mellow fruitfulness,
Close bosom friend of the maturing sun..."
From *To Autumn* by *John Keats*

Autumn has always been a wonderful time to me. Memories of those childhood days when the trees were red and golden and the hedges were loaded with fruit and berries were magical. It was also an important time during the war because here was free food with no ration books needed. It was a precious harvest to share with the birds and all we needed were jam jars and baskets to gather nature's gifts before the year came to an end.

We were taught diligently by the farmer's wife which wild foods were edible and which ones were poisonous and should never be touched. At six, I could tell the difference between the poisonous Bryony berries and vitamin rich rose hips and that the lethal berries of Lords and Ladies plant, Deadly Nightshade and red yew berries were strictly out of bounds.

Things that grew in abundance in the farm hedgerows and woods were elderberries, blackberries, rose hips, crab apples, beech and hazel nuts, tiny wild strawberries and hawthorn berries. Pies, jams, jellies and juices could all be made, restricted only by sugar rationing. During the war, people learned to enjoy foods less sweet than before but sugar quotas had to be balanced with honey and certain herbs from the garden that rendered sour fruits less bitter. For pies and desserts to eat immediately that was not a problem but for jams that needed to be kept it was important to accumulate sugar carefully to provide jams that kept. Earlier in the year, elderflowers were picked to make cordials. Runner beans were put in jars and packed with salt to preserve them for the winter. Each perfect cooking apple was wrapped in a piece of newspaper and packed in bowls or boxes. They would keep for several months.

There were no fridges or freezers then but our farmhouse had a specially designed pantry that was cool. It faced north, was slightly sunken and had a stone floor and grey slate shelves. It was frequently white-washed with lime wash, a natural antiseptic and of course there was no central heating then to infiltrate every room. The meat safe was a wooden cupboard with wire mesh doors to allow air in and keep the flies out.

In the autumn our little fingers were always stained with purple juice from blackberries and the kitchen smelled of the rich juices.

Our mother and grandmothers made jams, pies and jellies from our pickings for family use but the farmer's wife ran a small business from her side of the house. It was not only the wild fruits that were picked but the damsons, apples, pears, cherries and greengages that grew in the garden. Here, in vast pans on the wood burning stove in the farmhouse kitchen, she concocted the most astonishing variety of jams that even included such things as mangold-wurzels, from the fields. These were a type of beet with a large, yellowish root, really grown to feed the cattle and were shredded by large metal machines in the red brick barn. We loved to eat these crispy, raw shreds. When the fictional scarecrow character Wurzel Gummidge came on the scene in children's stories we all new exactly who he was.

One room in the farmhouse was called the long room. It had an enormous ingle nook fireplace with seats either side of the chimney and there was always a roaring fire. Fuel was free of course, sawn up from the dead, pruned or fallen trees in the wood and on the farm. The picture on the following page shows my father and Uncle Bob, complete with trilby hats, helping to saw the logs.

Down the centre of the room were long trestle tables. On Saturdays the room was turned into a tea house for ramblers and cyclists who came out from the town for a breath of country air. They were given giant pots of tea and home made bread and scones served with large dishes of the mysterious jams that had made the farmer's wife famous. In those days there was no need to put all the ingredients on a label so mangold-wurzels (sometimes known as mangel-wurzels), were the secret ingredient that made this wartime treat so delicious and cheap when combined with the fruits of the hedgerow.

The one fruit that I missed was the banana. Before the war, as a small child, they were one of my favourite foods. After Christmas, when we were

My father and Uncle Bob, complete with trilby hats, helping to saw the logs.

at the farm, my brother and I were given notepaper to write thank-you letters for our presents and I can remember one year starting every letter with "I wish I could have a banana"!

Chapter 12

THE VILLAGE SHOPS

"The Smith, a mighty man is he,
With large and sinewy hands;
And the muscles of his brawny arms
Are strong as iron bands."
From *The Village Blacksmith* by *Henry Wadsworth Longfellow*

Making do and mending was an art learned by everyone during the war. Children's dresses were made from skirts, hats and gloves were knitted from odd balls of wool so they contained many colours, and worn out socks were darned rather than being thrown away. One of the lessons at the village school was darning sock heels and we had little wooden mushrooms to push inside the sock as a frame to make darning easier.

At the far end of the village was a magic shop. Miss Morris had anything anybody wanted that could not be made at home, including the wooden darning mushrooms. Everything was hidden in a mass of boxes on shelves, in corridors and on every stair. Men's vests, hair curlers, tins of Spam or peaches, gardening equipment, washing powder, stationery, fishing equipment, all jostled for attention in the tiny shop that was squeezed into a small house.

Every bit of wall was covered in hand-written notes giving advice on diverse subjects and also several official wartime posters. They gave advice like **Careless Talk Costs Lives**, **Dig for Victory** and **Make Do and Mend**. One explained how to make children's clothes out of men's suits. I wondered what would happen when the men came out of the army and wanted to go back to work. Would there be advice on how to make men's suits out of children's outgrown clothing? **Walls have Ears** was funny because there was not an inch of free wall in her chaotic shop to fit even one small ear.

On Sunday, Miss Morris closed her shop and brought the village children to the long room for Sunday School. These were the village children who did not go to our little Catholic church. They not only sang hymns but also shared in the bread and jam which was a big attraction. I used to listen outside the large oak door and remember them singing and clapping to "I'm h-a-p-p-y, I'm h-a-p-p-y. I know I am, I'm sure I am, I'm h-a-p-p-y".

Each Christmas they had a party and invited Gerard and me. They were always surprised that we knew the words of their hymns and songs and we didn't like to admit that we had spent the rest of the year eavesdropping.

The only other shops in the village were a baker, a butcher, a post office with groceries, a cobbler and a blacksmith. In every shop there was always a chair by the counter for customers to rest while they waited to be served.

The baker's shop made all their own bread and there was always a wonderful smell pervading the street. The butcher sold locally killed meat from the surrounding farms and encouraged people to cook the cheaper cuts like oxtail, tripe, pig's cheek and various forms of offal. He also made sausages. They tasted good but probably contained all sorts of strange bits that would never have been eaten before the war.

The post office cum grocers took orders from everyone and they were delivered to homes by an errand boy on a bicycle. My mother had a little black book for writing her weekly order and I can remember her opening mantra every week as she sat by the fire and started to write – sugar, butter, bacon, marg, lard, now what? The rest of the list was hard because so many items were rationed or scarce and it took great ingenuity and skill to create nourishing meals for our household that had to feed not only my parents, my brother and me but also two grandmothers and two aunts.

Food rationing had started on January 9th 1940 and everyone was issued with a ration book full of coupons giving us the exact amount in ounces of butter, sugar and bacon from the shop. The shop keeper had to cut out the coupons in exchange for the goods. Later it was made simpler so that the shop could just stamp the coupon square.

Most foods were not pre-packed. Goods like sugar and biscuits were weighed and put into paper bags. Sweets went into rolled cones of paper that could be held easily in a child's hand. Sweets were rationed to a few ounces a week and Gerard and I had our own sweets jars on either side of the mantelpiece. Mine usually contained Dainty Dinah toffees and Gerard's had his favourite, boiled sweets, but we were only allowed to eat some after our main cooked meal of the day, which was normally at midday.

Sweet rationing was not lifted until some time after the war, on April 24th 1949.

An important craftsman in the village was the highly skilled cobbler, who specialised in anything made of leather, from footwear for humans to saddles and other leather items for the local horses. The walls of his shop were hung with vast sheets of leather, with soles and heels of various sizes cut out of them. On wires across the walls hung shoelaces of every length, probably saved from worn or outgrown shoes of his customers. He mended shoes and was also skilled at making them. Our family's leather shoes were solid and frequently mended as we all walked everywhere and strong footwear was essential in the unmade paths and muddy fields and woods.

Next door to the cobbler was the village blacksmith who repaired the metal shoes of the many local horses. Some of them were large Shire horses who worked on the farms pulling hay wagons and ploughs. Others were sophisticated riding horses that took part in annual gymkhanas, a highlight in the social life of the village. There were tractors but not every farm had one and many farmers relied on horses both for work on the farm and for their own transport. There was always the glow and intense heat of the huge furnace and the clang of hammers on metal coming from the blacksmith's workshop as he hammered the iron shoes into shape and nailed them onto the patient horses' feet.

Chapter 13

SILK, FUR AND FEATHERS

"If 'ifs' and 'ands' were pots and pans
There'd be no work for the tinkers..."
From *Manley* by *Thomas Love Peacock*

There was a wartime poster asking for old saucepans to be donated to make Spitfires, but in the country we had a saucepan mender who came round to repair old pans and kettles. He would put metal patches on the holes to seal them and they were surprisingly waterproof when he had fixed them so no Spitfires came from us.

Wedding dresses seen at the village church were wonderful. Parachutes to allow airmen to leap from planes were made of silk. After a parachute had landed it was not always suitable to be used again so many wonderful wedding dresses were fashioned out of used parachute silk and the floating, light material was just right to waft up the aisle. The grooms were often home for a short leave before going back to the front line so they wore their service uniforms.

Uncle Ted and Auntie Joan were married at Saint Francis of Assisi Church in Rising Lane, Baddesley Clinton while he was on leave from the army early in World

Uncle Ted and Auntie Joan.

45

War II. He had the luxury of wearing his own suit. The picture shows them after the wedding, at the entrance to Priest Park Farm house, showing the wonderful green-clipped privet that created an entrance to the front door. After Ted had returned to army service in Europe Joan stayed with us at the farm. Her first child, Joan, was born in Chadwick End and the picture on the right shows me, Auntie Joan's older sister

Mary and the new baby Joan, in the farmhouse garden with the ancient red brick barn in the background.

Ted was one of the fortunate ones that came back after the war and he used to tell us horrific stories about how they had to march waist deep through muddy fields on the continent and emerge covered in black leeches that sucked blood and had to be forced off the skin with salt water.

A short time after we had moved to the country, another uncle and aunt, my mother's brother Bob and his wife Dorothy and daughter Mary came to live in the village in a cottage at the top end of our fordrough, by the main road. Aunt kept hutches of beautiful Chinchilla rabbits. They were not only lovely pets but also provided food and fur. We all had warm, soft gloves made by our aunt from the warm, silky rabbit fur and they were essential in the bitter cold winters when walking or cycling to school. The rabbits also provided delicious pies and stews but they were treated well while they lived and were very much loved by all of us. Their garden also had what was known as the Sweetie Apple tree that in autumn was laden with tiny, green, very sweet apples that I have never found anywhere else. The branches hung down to the ground to create a perfect den underneath them and we spent many hours in there, with ready made lunch to hand. The cottage garden was also full of home grown vegetables and soft fruits – a virtual food store. During the war shops stopped selling flowers and concentrated on growing and selling fruit and vegetables. This meant that churches lacked flowers on the altar for

Cousin Mary.

special occasions so my aunt also grew beds of dahlias in her garden and took armfuls of the brightly coloured, exotic blooms to the church for weddings, christenings and feast days. The photograph on the previous page shows our cousin Mary sitting on the wall outside their cottage.

A luxury for all of us in the country was the feather bed mattresses. They were made of course from the feathers plucked from the farm's poultry when they were being prepared for the cooking pot. Every feather was saved for pillows, cushions and mattresses. It was wonderful to leap on the bed and just sink down into a soft, soft welcome. I was spoiled because since then I have never been able to sleep on a hard bed.

Stockings for women were either scarce or unobtainable. Many young women would paint their legs with watered down gravy browning. In those days, real stockings had a seam that had to be kept straight up the back of the leg. With gravy brown legs, the seam was painted on using neat gravy browning and they hoped it did not rain while they were going to work or to the dance in the village hall.

Christmas decorations were easy to find. We just picked berried holly from the farm and stuck a sprig behind every picture on the wall. Our streamers were special and very unusual and could only be made in wartime. When we were picking fruit, or harvesting the corn, we often found strips of silver paper lying in the fields or caught in the brambles. I have never discovered what they were but they were dropped from aeroplanes flying overhead. They were about two inches wide and shimmered in the sunshine. We gathered them all and made them into silver streamers for decorating the living room. Each one could be made into a loop and the loops joined together and stuck down. No streamers since have pleased us as much as those.

Christmas cards and presents of book marks were made from flowers and leaves that we had gathered during the year and pressed in the pages of books. Years later, after the war, we often opened a book and out would flutter the odd leaf or sprig that had been pressed and forgotten.

If we needed special shops like the chemist or outfitters we had to go to the next village. There was one bus a week there, on a Thursday, so it was always full. If we missed the one back it was a long walk.

The doctor's surgery was also in the next village so all our appointments had to be on a Thursday. If we were ill though, he always came to visit us and he was a regular visitor to both our grandmothers. Grandmothers also had their own home-made cures as well – like goose grease on brown paper for a bad chest and warm olive oil, only obtainable at the chemist in those days, for earache and dry skin. Gargles were made from sage and thyme that grew in the farm garden and the farmer's wife knew of many cures that could be brewed up from fresh herbs.

Very occasionally, we took the single-decker village bus all the way into Birmingham where it stopped in the Bull Ring, right outside the spired church of Saint Martin in the Bull Ring. At that time it was a busy market full of characters with their own sales calls. It was a good place to get cheap fresh fruit and vegetables, and at the end of the day everything was reduced in price. We could not take advantage of the special offers though because by that time the village bus home had long gone. In the doorway of one shop there was always a little lady selling brown paper carrier bags and singing loudly to shoppers "'Andy Carrier. Get yer 'andy carrier."

One man with a little wooden wagon on wheels parked by the kerb sold lisle stockings with seams up the back. There were no nylons then. My aunt bought a pair and thought she had a bargain until she tried them on and there was a ladder all the way up the leg. She took them back the following week and the stall-holder replaced them, saying, "Sorry luv – I thought yer father was a fireman"!

A man on a soap box who was known as Holy Jo seemed to be giving a permanent religious sermon and he was always surrounded by a crowd of listeners and hecklers.

In 1941 a bomb hit the church and many surrounding buildings also suffered bomb damage but still the market kept going and the resilience of the shoppers was amazing. A bomb was not going to stop them going to market.

Chapter 14

ITMA AND ALL THAT

"Child! Do not throw this book about;
Refrain from the unholy pleasure
Of cutting all the pictures out.
Preserve it as your greatest treasure."
From *Bad Child's Book of Beasts* by *Hilaire Belloc*

There was no television, record player, computer, CD player or mobile phone in those days so all our entertainment was either from live performances or the choice of the BBC Home Service or the Forces Programme (which became the Light Programme) on the wireless. It sat on the dining table, a beautiful, polished wood box. Favourites were Workers' Playtime and ITMA – a comedy show with Tommy Handley that stood for *It's That Man Again*. His cleaner, Mrs. Mop, would arrive with a loud bang of the door and say "Can I do you now sir?" and Colonel Chinstrap represented the army. I never understood what the ITMA character Funf was but we all loved to copy his odd voice saying, "Dis is Funf speaking".

Another show featured Elsie and Doris Waters, two comediennes known as Gert and Daisy, who were also great fun. They were the sisters of actor Jack Warner OBE who later became PC George Dixon in the film *The Blue Lamp* and on television as *Dixon of Dock Green*. His real surname was Waters.

Wartime special programmes were the *Radio Doctor*, with Doctor Charles Hill, whose distinctive voice gave good advice on how to keep healthy during rationing and *Kitchen Front*, a daily cookery programme coping with shortages and making the most of things like dried egg, Spam and corned beef. Recipes varied from artichokes in cheese to oatmeal sausages, stuffed cabbage and Woolton Pie. Lord Woolton was the wartime Minister of Food and his recommended pie was a mixture of any sort of stewed vegetables available with the juices thickened with oatmeal and a topping of potato pastry.

Gerard and I loved *Children's Hour* that ran from 5.00pm until 6.00pm every weekday on the BBC Home Service. It included *Toy Town* with Larry the Lamb, Mr. Mayor and Dennis the Dachshund, a German sausage dog. There was also a Policeman called Ernest, Mr Inventor and Mr Growser the Grocer. Every child at the school could imitate the shaky talk of Larry the Lamb bleating *"Oh Mr. Mayor Sir."*

Our mother had been an accomplished pianist before the war and one of the things she missed most at the farm was her piano. She never lost the skill though, even after so many years, and when we returned to Sutton Coldfield after the war she would keep us entranced on a Sunday afternoon with Mendelssohn's *Songs Without Words* and the works of Johann Sebastian Bach.

At the farm, one of the great pleasures on a Sunday, after a hearty roast lunch, was to listen to the afternoon orchestral concert on the Home Service as we sat round the blazing log and coal fire. It laid the foundation for my love of music, one of the mainstays and great comforts of the rest of my life. While listening to music and staring into the fire, my vivid imagination ran riot and I could see pictures in the flames. I had also developed a love of poetry through my parents and encouragement at the little school and I started to write my own. One of the first was on such a late afternoon in winter, with flames leaping round logs gathered from the farm woods. I started to scribble what came into my head as we listened to a Mozart Piano Concerto. It is not a great poem but it was my first attempt and the words just seemed to arrive on the page.

Travels by the fire
When the curtains are drawn on a wintry night
And I look in the fire which is merry and bright,
I do not see living creatures,
But castles and caves and things like that,
Or coal burned the image of Grandpa's top hat,
Or maybe people's features.

When I enter into one of those caves
I imagine outside there are surging waves
For I'm a pirate bold.

I capture ships from far off lands
And eat my meals with blood-stained hands,
As men in days of old.

But when I see castles I think of kings
And diamond tiaras or ruby rings
Or perhaps the Young Pretender.
Then away from the dreams where my thoughts may roam
I land by the fire in the lounge at home
With my feet upon the fender.

I loved playing with words from when I was very young. With a father who was a journalist and a book reviewer, my brother and I had the luxury as children of books, stories and poetry read to us, given as presents and also arriving in his weekly review pile. Every week while we were in the country our father would also bring us a library book from the old Margaret Street Library in the centre of Birmingham. Two favourites when I was nine were *The Jungle Book* and *Puck of Pook's Hill* by Rudyard Kipling. At the weekend my special treat was the weekly children's magazine *Sunny Stories* by Enid Blyton. Many children had poems published in there and it was full of stories by Enid Blyton herself and amusing snippets and pictures. It inspired me to read her books, *The Famous Five* series and many others and I loved to curl up in an armchair or in bed with a book.

Gerard used to get a publication called *The Children's Newspaper* that was full of news, stories and competitions. Edited by Arthur Mee for more than half a century until his death in 1943, it looked like a real newspaper. Arthur Mee (seen on the right) had also created the *Children's Encyclopaedia*. As a child of a journalist who was always surrounded by newspapers, it made my brother feel very grown-up to have this paper and it featured real news stories, including those about the war, so was educational as well as being fun and presented just for children.

We used to be encouraged to read aloud to our grandmothers too. We thought then it was to help and entertain them but I realise now that it was our parents' way of getting us to read, enjoy and become fluent with words as much as possible and it also gave our grandmothers the enjoyment of our company. My two grandmothers also tried to teach me to knit and sew but it was a struggle and I was never as good as they were. There was a hand sewing machine in the farm living room and between them they made us all some wonderful clothes out of bits and scraps.

My brother loved making plywood models of ships and planes from kits that he was given for Christmas and birthday presents. Some of them were really impressive and demanded skilled fingers, hours of patience and a lot of glue.

Card games were another form of entertainment in the long winter evenings and the whole family would gather round the fire to play snap, rummy, whist and strip Jack naked.

We enjoyed painting and drawing but I struggled at that. Our cousin Mary, who lived in the cottage at the top of the fordrough, was artistic. She had the gift of being able to draw and paint that I always admired but could never achieve. Years later she became a professional artist but we loved to see her work that was a natural, inborn talent that could not be learned.

Games in the school playground were very traditional. Bulldog, Tipcat, Rounders, Hopscotch, Cat and Mouse, Simon Says, Polly on the Mopstick and endless varieties with skipping ropes kept us amused when the weather was fine enough to be outside.

Skipping rhymes varied from Silk, Satin, Muslin, Rags to Tinker, Tailor, Soldier, Sailor, Richman, Poorman, Beggarman, Thief. **R**ichard **O**f **Y**ork **G**ave **B**attle **I**n **V**ain was a history rhyme that also taught us the order of the colours of the rainbow.

Learning rhymes and songs by rote is sometimes frowned upon now but for us they were a basis for knowledge that stayed for life. The verse giving the list of Kings and Queens in rhyme gave us the complete chronological list from William the Conquerer to George VI, who was our King then, and I have welcomed that list on many occasions. Here it is, updated, with our present Queen added.

Mnemonics of Royalty

Willie, Willie, Harry, Stee,
Harry, Dick, John, Harry Three.
One, two, three Neds, Richard two,
Henry four, five, six, then who?

Edward four, five, Dick the Bad,
Henrys twain then Ned the Lad.
Mary, Bessie, James the Vain,
Charlie, Charlie, James again.

William and Mary, Anna Gloria,
Four Georges, William and Victoria,
Edward the Seventh next and then
George the Fifth in 1910.

Edward the Eighth soon abdicated
And so a George was reinstated.
Elizabeth Two now rules our state,
While Charles the Third just has to wait.

There were special skipping songs for various seasonal celebrations. The day before Lent began we used to sing this that originally came from my mother who learned it at her school in Birmingham when she was young. The name of any lane can be substituted in the fourth line. We changed it to the lane leading to the village school.

Pancake Day
Pancake Day, Pancake Day,
If you don't give us holiday we'll all run away.
Where shall we run to?
Down Rising Lane,
Here comes teacher with a big fat cane.

During the holidays of course, Gerard and I and our cousin Mary had the freedom of the whole farm to wander, climb trees, build tree houses and explore. One day, with a group of friends, we discovered what looked like a beautiful wooden carving full of miniature holes, in the root of a Weeping Willow Tree. We carefully lifted it out and took it back home, hoping to show it to the adults later. In the meantime we stored it in the woodshed outside the farmer's kitchen.

Unfortunately, it happened to be a wasp's nest and as the wasps hatched out in the heat of the carved logs, they discovered with delight that the farmer's wife was making jam in the kitchen. Mayhem ensued as she cried "Wasps" (pronounced to rhyme with clasps) and tried to slay them with her wooden spoon. We were not very popular that day and I think that she wondered why it was ever a good idea to have "townies" to stay during the war.

Chapter 15

ALL CHANGE

"The pen is mightier than the sword."

Cows were an important part of the farm. During the day they were in the fields, grazing, but at the end of the day they were brought in to the brick built cow sheds next to the farmhouse and their comforting, soft calls could be heard at night.

We were taught how to milk them and when calves came we were given the strange sensation of putting our hands into their moist, sucking mouths.

There was always fresh milk but unfortunately, my brother developed a TB gland in his neck from the unpasteurised milk and had to spend some time in Birmingham Children's Hospital having it removed. Visiting was restricted but sometimes Mother could go on the Thursday bus or the train into Birmingham to see him.

After three years at the little local school our parents decided to send us to larger schools nearer to the centre of Birmingham. We had both learned to ride bicycles, which was essential for getting to the railway station one and a half miles away to catch a steam train. It was good fun in the summer but when winter came the ride home was often freezing. Our Chinchilla rabbit fur gloves, made by our Aunt, saved icy fingers. We were just glad to get home to a blazing log fire and a hearty meal but our days of freedom on the farm were curtailed. We longed for the holidays so that we could run free again.

The change of school was dramatic for me. After the small, intimate classes of the village school I was in uniform, with many other girls. It was compulsory to wear a hat when we were outside in uniform – straw hats in summer and navy felt ones in winter, with the school hatband and badge above the brim.

The beautiful copperplate writing I had learned in the country had to be forgotten and a rigid, straight up and down with no loops style adopted. My writing never adapted well and is still a hotch-potch of styles.

Steam trains and stations were exciting and I learned the words and slogans on the advertisements and posters on the walls and in the waiting rooms. They were like the old nursery rhymes we recited when we were younger. One poster I loved was on the station over the wooden bench where I sat waiting for the train home from school. It was an advertisement for a fountain pen. At the new school we were sometimes allowed to write with fountain pens that we could fill up with ink and my first one was a birthday present from my parents, together with sheets of blotting paper to dry the ink (and often the stray blots) on the page. I felt so grown up.

The advertisement said:

> **They came as a boon and a blessing to men,**
> **The Pickwick, the Owl and the Waverley pen.**

Another, on every station, asked: **Is your journey really necessary?** Our schools might not have appreciated it if we had taken that literally and stopped at home.

There were no corridors in the trains then. Whichever carriage we got in we had to stay in and there were just two long seats facing each other. Above some of them were relics of better days, faded coloured photographs or paintings of distant seaside destinations from the pre-war days of holidays by train. There were mountain scenes and rails running along side the beaches, rocks and coastline, all featuring a train speeding along with its trails of steam obliterating some of the scenery. It all looked so romantic. I longed to go to one of these wonderful places but it would be years before peace arrived and we could venture to the coast again.

As 1945 got underway so did the idea grow that peace was on the horizon. My parents decided that we could go back to our old home in Sutton Coldfield and resume normal life again. For them it would be a relief but for Gerard and me it would mean losing our freedom and precious wild country life that we had absorbed and relished for our growing years.

In early spring we were home, back to our familiar house in Sutton Coldfield. It was fun to re-discover it and find familiar things in the garden and surrounding area – memories of a very young child – but still vivid. I recalled the red-tiled hall floor on which we had all stood on that fateful day to hear the announcement of war and here we all were, five years later, facing peace.

On May 13th 1945, as Big Ben struck 3.00pm, London was awash with crowds round Whitehall and The Mall and elsewhere and the whole country waited with baited breath for the broadcast on the wireless that was to announce the end of conflict.

The Prime Minister Winston Churchill's booming voice said that the war in Europe would end at midnight. "Advance Britannia!" he cried. Gathering crowds outside and people in their own homes shouted, "Long live the cause of freedom. God save the King."

On that evening, on the balcony of the Ministry of Health in London, the Prime Minister appeared in his Homburg hat and siren suit. A band played *For He's a Jolly Good Fellow* and then Churchill himself conducted the crowd who sang *Land of Hope and Glory* to the music of Sir Edward Elgar.

It was all heady stuff and by this time, five years after the start of our rural adventure, we understood what was going on and joined in the excitement. The newspapers next day were full of pictures of the event, with happy faces, jubilant, flag waving crowds and dancing in the streets. The news on the wireless, at long last, was good news.

Back home, in The Royal Town of Sutton Coldfield, we celebrated after that with rejoicing, dancing and music round the World War I war memorial in King Edward's Square outside the Town Hall with the Mayor of Sutton Coldfield and the councillors joining the celebrations. To see every adult smiling and cheering was a tonic after years of grey, solemn sadness and worry. Just as I had sensed, five years before, the dread and horror of the adults as war was announced, so on this day, Gerard and I could feel the elation and relief of our families and the whole nation.

Food was still rationed, there was a shortage of everything we needed and our clothes were old but it was not important then. Peace was the greatest thing we had and nothing else mattered.

It was the end of an era, the end of our idyllic rural life and the start of normality tinged with magical memories that have stayed with us for ever.

King George VI did not forget the children when the war ended. Boys and girls received their own certificate from him, recognising the trials of being a child in time of war.

Looking back into the last century to those magical times in the country, through the eyes of a young child, I realise that we were privileged to have had such freedom when our country was gripped by war and tragedy.

My memories remain vivid of those fields and woods where we wandered as children and learned to love the animals, insects and the profusion of wild flowers. I see them now, as the English poet William Wordsworth did in

8th June, 1946

TO-DAY, AS WE CELEBRATE VICTORY, I send this personal message to you and all other boys and girls at school. For you have shared in the hardships and dangers of a total war and you have shared no less in the triumph of the Allied Nations.

I know you will always feel proud to belong to a country which was capable of such supreme effort; proud, too, of parents and elder brothers and sisters who by their courage, endurance and enterprise brought victory. May these qualities be yours as you grow up and join in the common effort to establish among the nations of the world unity and peace.

George R.I

his poem *The Daffodils*, when he reminisced, "they flash upon that inward eye", looking back to a world that is vanishing and needs to be rescued from the ravages of progress.

This patchwork of memories and pictures ends with a poem I wrote as an adult when I realised that those flowers were disappearing from our countryside and I have put the cry for help into the voices of the flowers themselves. Words in bold lettering in the poem are the names of English wild flowers.

Cry of the Wild Flowers

Road cutters slash the rural green of England
And **Poppies** bleed beside the fresh cut swards.
Wounds of the motorways gape wide. Earth groans
While diggers slice the ground like seering swords.

Nature's nurse shrouds the sores with **Queen-Anne's-Lace**
To curtain off the gashed and weeping ground.
Self-heal and **Tansy** try to stem the pace
And **Stitchwort** sets to sew the septic wound.

Bluebells toll loud as Mother Nature cries
To see the scars that creep across her way.
Oak trees with wildlife's generations fall;
Not even **Lilies** can allay decay.

Bring out the **Bugle**! **Lords-and-Ladies** shout!
Bedstraw sleep not while earthy beds they sever.
Columbines, shed tears of sadness out.
Eye-bright, come see – your home has gone forever.

"**Forget-me-not**", the English meadow pleads.
Pink **Ladysmocks** call, "We're too young to die",
While cars stream by on tissue-scarred hard roads
And England's heart lies crushed, uprooted, dry.

One day, we'll join the flowers' angry cry
When there's no country left, no rural scene.
But then, too late, no **Rattle, Rocket, Sage,**
Will save our **Traveller's Joy**, our **Thyme** lost green.

Mary Daniels

THE END